When Watermelon had Seeds

Thought-provoking poems by

Edmond Bruneau

ISBN: 978-1-936769-14-8
Library of Congress Control Number: 2025914681

Cover Design: Edmond Bruneau
Editor: Donna Lange

Previous books by Edmond Bruneau
Prescription for Advertising – 1986
Colors of My Within – 2011
New Hues and Past Tales – 2016
The Totem – 2018
Walla Walla Sweet – 2021
Sip and Savor – 2023
Soul of the Song – 2025

Lyricist for:
Robot Raven's Greatest Hits - Part One – 2015
Robot Raven's Greatest Hits - Part Two – 2016
Life Goes On by Robot Raven – 2017
Set to Soar by Robot Raven – 2018
Robot Raven Rockers – 2018
Kick Back Relax by Robot Raven – 2020
Sunflower 69 by Whistlewit – 2022
Country Cousins by The Cow Cats – 2023

For my partner in life,
Donna Lange.

You make great moments glitter
and tough moments tolerable.
Plus, an editor extraordinaire.

Grateful for your love, every day.

FORWARD

This new collection is my sixth published book of poetry. 141 original poems and one short story.

When Watermelon had Seeds is a metaphor for my observation of the world. I remember a place which rarely exists any longer — and cannot help but to compare it with things as they are now.

The first 99 pages are basically a poem potpourri – an assortment of observations and memories I hope you'll find enjoyable, thought-provoking and insightful, with a few fun wordplays thrown in here and there.

Page 100 begins a look at the holidays and the four seasons, beginning with the New Year — continuing all the way to the Christmas season and an unusual letter to Santa Claus.

Page 130 begins with a nod to nature and ends appropriately with a sunset.

Then, beginning on *page 141,* topics become socially-conscious and political. So, consider this fair warning if you are not open to reading my poetic personal point of view.

Last, but not certainly least, is a short story I wrote awhile ago, but published here for the first time. *Why Dogs Hate Cats* is the missing Mother Goose tale that plainly explains why these two species have a natural animosity toward each other.

It is my hope, in the human world, we can avoid such antagonism and build bridges of friendship — a better future for all of us.

Edmond Bruneau

TABLE OF CONTENTS

When Watermelon had Seeds

Yesteryear.
Collecting sand dollars
while walking the beach.
Small plastic shovel and tin metal pail –
ocean water and imagination
build a sandcastle.

Striking out toward precarious peril,
we would hold hands and
walk into the surf waist high,
jumping waves to avoid
them going over our heads.
Sand in swim trunks a certainty.

It was nearly dinnertime
when aromatic lighter fluid
soaked coals suddenly became
a flaming inferno. Sizzle and smell
of hamburgers and hot dogs
from grill to hungry appetites.

Summer sunshine fades to dusk.
Campfire embers just right
to roast marshmallows on a stick.
The trick – golden brown perfection
without falling off or becoming
an accidental torch.

Thongs before flip flops.
Inner tubes before floaties.
Tanning orange with Coppertone.®
Root beer popsicles. Ice cream dixie cups.
Dime store inflatable beach balls.
And spitting watermelon seeds at each other.

"It is better to fail in originality than to succeed in imitation."
– Herman Melville

Original

To be original
is not only
a passion,
it's my
essential truth.

Purposely.
Not a
plagiarist,
fraud or
copycat.

In fact,
I do not
ever intend
to imitate
or borrow.

I strive to
be authentic.
Genuine,
Innovative.
Imaginative.

Any resemblance
to other works –
strictly
coincidental or
unintentional.

To succeed
in imitation
would be
ARTificial.
Plastic.

Whether
succeed or fail –
unimportant compared
to the value of
my virtue.

I am the
builder
with bricks
made of words.
Solid foundation.

Structures that
stand against
the sands of time.
With pride,
they are mine.

Spark of Madness

We're only given a little spark of madness.
Ours to use or lose.
Way to see past sadness.
Amplification for the muse.

Spark illuminates dark.
Visualizes beyond norm.
Extraordinary embarks
toward a journey transformed.

Spark – a flicker, a flare,
a gleam, a glint, a glow.
Key to being aware.
Humdrum overthrown.

Madness – a bit of lunacy
mixed with regular routine.
Allowing once blind to see
beyond the hills and trees.

We're only given a little spark of madness.
Enough to light a fire.
Kindling blaze caress.
New directions to aspire.

Yet, there's still time
to create poems with reason,
perhaps with rhyme.
Songs still to be sung as they align to shine.

I am muddled together,
with cable, cords and twine
and continue to be the man I am –
enduring heart and mind.

Be Your Art

It's inside you –
your special gift.
Unique as you are,
poised to uplift.

Whatever you're good at
that's where to start.
Share with others and
it becomes your art.

Sculpture or painting.
Poetry or prose.
Song or symphony
aptly composed.

Architecture. Theater.
Interior design.
Photography. Cinema.
Cooking with wine.

Working with children.
Pampering pets.
Quilting, carving, crochet –
So many vignettes.

Be the art inside you.
Add to the fabric of humanity.
Send your gift into the universe
with personal originality.

"Your character is your destiny"
– Heraclitus of Ephesus (c. 535 BC – 475 BC)

Character

Invisible, but
everyone sees it.
Impression made
on purpose or not.

Only way to gain
influence over how
people perceive you –
have character in the first place.

Be the person
you'd like as a friend.
Think of others
besides yourself.

People won't remember
how much money you had
or plethora of possessions.
Especially when you're gone.

What they'll remember is
how your deeds and actions
made a difference to them.
In both head and heart.

Be authentic.
Realize the universe
doesn't revolve around you.
Define your destiny.

"If I had my life to live over again, I would have made a rule to read some poetry and listen to some music at least once every week."
– Charles Darwin, author of ***The Origin of the Species***

Evolution Revolution

Darwin once said
survival is neither
intelligence or strength,
but adaptability.

Music and poetry
separates us from
monkey to man.
Makes us more human.

Adapt to change,
one thing.
Adopt new habits,
another.

Arts and science exist
to help us adapt better.
Our species survival
depends on it.

New habits like
listening to music
or reading poetry
is change within.

Developing
fresh interests –
a missing link
in evolution.

Doesn't it make
sense to enhance
quality of life during
natural selection?

Why not
enjoy the process
while fulfilling the
evolutionary cycle?

Mumbo Jumbo

Some people,
maybe many –
believe poetry
to be a lot of
mumbo jumbo.

To them,
it probably is.
Cannot make
hide nor hair
of its contents.

They unilaterally
distain poetry.
Poison to them.
Pariah in
written form.

Lump all
poets together
into one
heinous group.
Avoid at all costs.

But what if I reveal
there are secrets
hidden in poetry.
Created for those
who appreciate the art.

There is wisdom.
Humor. Insight.
Awareness.
Personal growth.
Appreciation of nature.

Presented in
clever form.
Words woven
together
like a tapestry.

Sometimes rhyme.
Occasionally silly.
Always from
true intentions.
Mumbo jumbo it's not.

It just wasn't meant
for them.

I've learned that one should keep his words both soft and tender,
because tomorrow he may have to eat them.
 – Andy Rooney, commentator on CBS 60 Minutes

Word Supper

Eating my words. Fine.
Not a delicious dine.

Hors d'oeuvres –
participle preserves.

Simile soup
like goulash goop.

Adjective appetizer
with adverb herbs.

Topical salad –
prepositional pallet.

Main course,
grammar endorsed.

Couple of nouns
to nibble down.

Metaphor munch –
crispy crunch.

Declarative dessert,
exclamation alert.

Indigestion irruption.
Vowel obstruction.

Anguish

Creeps up on me when I have
a question with no answer.
Frustrating not to understand –
letting my thoughts meander.

Inquiry with silence.
Partially paranoid.
How do I deal
with data devoid?

Question without resolution,
rebuttal or remark.
One can surmise, but perhaps
not even be in the ballpark.

Have a hundred guesses.
Most likely all are wrong,
If answer does come forward
why did it take so long?

Yes, it's my anguish.
Possessed in a world unknown.
Question with no answer.
Impossible to atone.

I don't enjoy the feelings.
Agony. Misery. Grief.
All because I do not find
the reply for my relief.

Something we all live with.
Things we do not know.
Striving to fill in the blanks.
Surviving the status quo.

*"Stop leaving and you will arrive. Stop searching and you will see.
Stop running away and you will be found."* – Lao Tzu

You Are Here

I'm reminded of red circle
on a large map sign
showing the location
where you are and
other points of interest.

You Are Here.

In actuality, it means more
than standing in a red circle.
You are here at this moment,
physically, mentally, emotionally.
It is literally your NOW.

You Are No Where Else BUT Here.

At that precise moment,
the sign is absolutely correct.
Perhaps as accurate as
a stopped clock being
right twice a day.

You WERE Here

You move on to one
of the points of interest
and discover another map
with a red circle in a
different spot of the sign.

You Are Now Here

You look back on the map
to where you had been,
which looks a lot like
all the other areas
without the red circle.

Wherever You Go, You Are Here

Don't really need a sign
to tell you that simple fact.
Any place you go, you are
there at that moment.
Arriving, then leaving.

Onto Another Here

Fact remains that
you can't actually
leave here because
here is your only constant.
It's the only thing that remains true.

You Are Here

Be here, now, is the electrical jolt
we all need to remember that
we are alive, heart beating,
lungs breathing, mind thinking,
sensitively feeling the world around us.

I Am Here

We don't require a red circle
to remind us that we get a finite
amount of precious moments.
We choose to use them here –
otherwise, we wouldn't be anywhere.

Friendly Goodbye

So gracious while
we're in your company.
Reminiscent of our
valuable time before.

Time spent together
seriously kindhearted.
Richness of love
unable to ignore.

Time has come
for us to leave.
Our turn to head out.
Depart your welcoming door.

Leaving with gratitude.
With thanks. Appreciation.
Won't delay our time away –
will be back for more rapport.

Kaleidoscope

My kaleidoscope
imagination
draws inspiration
from constantly changing views –
plethora of hues.

No mirrors, prisms
reflections, optics.
Peer deep into topics
beyond what's known.
Innovation's home.

Where new ideas
come from.
Opposite humdrum.
Birth of original thought.
Dawn the universe brought.

Twist the dial.
Examine different way.
One more dragon to slay.
Notion awoke.
My mental kaleidoscope.

Poetic Justice

*Sleep tight, don't let
the bedbugs bite.*

Not exactly a
heavenly goodnight.
Tepid attempt
to assist sleep.

Peevish prequel
for dreamland.
Smudged sendoff
to slumber.

Journey of
forty winks.
Now a
manic trance.

Centaur in elevator.
Dressed for the occasion.
In full
pest control regalia.

Bedbugs be gone.
Poetic justice.

Silhouette

Like a permanent shadow,
silhouette edges determine
the shape of what it resembles
in its own two-dimensional way.

Umbrella without protection.
Bulb minus incandescence.
Portrait clear of humanity.
Bungalow with no square feet.

A paradox, really.
Appearing to be
something more
than it really is.

Shallow. Superficial.
Flat. Depthless.
Only the surface matters.
Nothing more inside.

There are people
who nefariously share
the same qualities –
focusing on appearance.

No deep conversations.
Obsessed with themselves.
Uncompassionate.
Victim mentality.

They are but a silhouette –
resembling a human being
without dimension.
Sans a soul.

Tattoo

Her tattoo was a parrot –
seemed a little gauche.
Grass skirt at her waistline
she loved the hula most.

Came from the islands.
Needed no rehearsal.
Now living on the coast –
thinking about a reversal.

Could she take the tattoo
and make it more obscure?
Didn't produce the flattery
she expected from the allure.

A mistake, she conceded.
Could it be extracted?
Salient vision of the bird
aggravated and distracted.

"Make the parrot a butterfly"
as she laid on the parlor table.
Yet, it was not meant to be
as the artist was unable.

Said it must be removed
by a laser and a surgeon.
Next time think it through
and avoid such an aversion.

Astral Allegory

Clairvoyant
conjecture.
Soul
from stars
into
new realm.
Knowledge
of beginning.

Illuminating
information.
Question
of balance –
exist to
assist
others with
their dreams.

While also
developing
self
enhancement
through
changes
and fireworks
we call life.

Time passes
and the
body grows
geriatric.
Going home,
without ceremony
but with
a twinkle.

Monotony

Humdrum day.
Same old thing.
Tedious tedium.
Stillness sings.

Insipid routine.
Predictable play.
Boring banality.
Tiresome souffle.

Lack of adventure.
Titillation. Stimuli.
Passion. Dynamics.
Elation denied.

Not always exciting.
Not always a thrill.
Some days, just familiar.
Doldrums distilled.

We all have those days –
Stuffy, stodgy and tame.
Ho-hum, uninspired.
Nothing to proclaim.

If it wasn't for monotony,
it'd be a thrill a minute.
At the edge of your seat –
Whirlwind ticket.

Roller coaster rides
always come to an end.
Monotony, a respite.
Rejuvenating friend.

Forget Me Not

Hard drive failing
after many
years of operation.

Fragmented recovery.
Error messages.
Corrupted data.

Started with
longer processing
for answers.

Until it began
searching
without finding.

Sluggish performance.
One day,
no recall at all.

Suddenly strangers
surround – acting
like they know you.

It's even
more difficult for
forgotten friends, relatives.

Who can no longer
share past memories
or mutual experiences.

It's the saddest disease,
Alzheimer's. Familiar
becomes unacquainted.

Bouquet of *Forget Me Nots*
greeted with an empty stare –
as the flowers wither at bedside.

In the Palm of My Hand

She takes my hand –
studies the lines
especially where
they intersect.

Looks at my life line.
Head line. Heart line.
Fate line. Sun line.
Palm ponderous.

Palmistry probes
fleshy inner hand,
determining the
type of mount.

Investigates finger
length and shape.
Thumb, index
middle, ring and pinky.

After all analysis,
gypsy explains in length
what it all means
for my fortune.

Pleasant entertainment
without crystal ball.
Past, present
and future foretold.

Sounds a lot like me.
Or thousands of others
gullible enough to
believe generalizations.

My fate ahead –
my days tomorrow,
unfortunately not
in the palm of my hand.

The wind that fills my sails propels,
but I am the helmsman. – George Meredith

Self Portrait

Color me red.
For love.
For anger
against injustice.

Color me green.
For healing.
Universal signal
for go.

Color me yellow.
Illustrating
caution and
sensitivity.

Color me blue.
Symbolizing optimism.
Blue skies.
Enthusiasm.

Mix up hues
of kindness and curiosity.
Don't paint a smile.
One is already there.

It's ok to
color outside of the lines.
Not a true self-portrait
unless you do.

From the palette,
paint on positivity.
Doesn't have to be perfect.
Certainly, I am not.

We're all made up
of the colors we are.
How we draw or paint them
is what the world observes.

Rumor has It

I heard...
Someone told me...
Did you know...?

In a whisper,
a sound and solid
reputation
can crumble.

It's not
the truth
but a
false rumor.

A rumor
so deliciously
decadent
it must be shared.

Shared
behind one's back.
In muttered
conversations.

Careful to
spread it about,
away from
victim's ears.

Rumors morph into
false perception.
For many,
perception is reality.

How can one
battle such
cold blooded
backstabbing?

Especially when
the trusting soul
is the
last to know?

You can't.
Even if one
discovers the source –
misinformation has spread.

Certainly,
it's not feasible
to confront
everyone who heard.

Realize it is not
worth the energy.
Childish,
elementary school behavior.

Continue to
live life with
truth
and integrity.

Be yourself.
If it's nonsense
there is
nothing to defend.

Ruby Red Slippers

Click your heels
three times and say:
"There's no place like home."
"There's no place like home."
"There's no place like home."

If fairy tales true
and magic holds,
you're transported
to a place where
reassurance resides.

You're embraced.
And loved.
Protected from the
hostility and hassles
of the outside world.

How nice it would be
to travel there
in a moment's notice.
Flight from trepidation
and disillusionment.

Then again –
are we meant to
live in a safe bubble
every time we encounter
danger or difficulty?

Flee instead of stand?
Evade or persuade?
Avoid or face fear?
Retreat than fight?
Leave or continue living?

Too easy escape –
clicking heels and
reciting incantation.
Dealing with detriment
part of a soul's education.

People Change

In my nostalgic mind
I cling to the idea that
you are the same as
the last time we met.
Truth is, we all are
different than yesterday.

Most of the time,
it's so subtle
one doesn't notice.
Perhaps more apparent
when a greater measure
of time has passed.

Heraclitus claimed, *"No one ever steps in the
same river twice, for it's not the same water
and they're not the same person."*
Be it age, fear, solitude,
loss, pride or control –
factors of change influence our journey.

I make peace with the fact
that you are as you are today.
A daily fresh look at all the
cast of characters in life –
to see if the combination still works
that unlocks our pathway.

Sticks & Stones

It's true.
Sticks and stones
can break bones.
So will
other things like
bullets and bombs.

Said in reference
to flinging
words or names
which in reality
do not cause
bones to break.

Yet words
can cause
a broken spirit,
discouragement
or worse –
a broken heart.

Insults, verbal abuse,
shame, scorn, slander –
emotionally detrimental
as a
stick in the gut
or stone to skull.

Let's update this silly
children's rhyme
to recognize
words do cause pain...
Perhaps worse than
a poke or punch.

*Sticks and stones can break my bones
but words can hurt me more.
Things you say don't go away –
impossible to ignore.
When you try to bad mouth me,
in time you'll get your due.
A finger pointed my direction
leaves three pointing back at you!*

Fringe of Superficial

The limited frequency
we dial each other in.
Narrow bandwidth.
Controlled. Constrained.
Depthless conversations
avoid anything profound.

We swim in the
shallow waters of safety,
playing in puddles
of unmeaningful minutia.
Without worry of drowning
in a sea of particulars.

There have been times
attempting to stretch
the restricted limitations,
only to reach resistance.
Stay in the lane.
Don't diverge from path.

Perhaps it's self-preservation.
Beyond the scope
of discussion could be
too painful or uncomfortable
to be exposed
in the light of day.

Here we sit, with empty smiles.
Nothing but small talk.
Street appraisal without
ever venturing inside.
Longing to exceed the
fringe of superficial.

Careless Whispers

Quietly, so only
another could hear.
Whisper's damage
fed into an ear.

Detrimental details
passed on along.
Truth or taunt when
right becomes wrong?

Be it gossip or hearsay.
Slander or scandal.
Someone gets an earful.
Scuttlebutt shamble.

Rumormonger
repeats referendum.
An agenda besides
contaminating venom?

Whispers heard –
believed blatantly.
Communication
quite cowardly.

A mutter, a mumble.
Innuendo or sigh.
Insinuation misinformation.
Shameless shanghai.

Watching a whisper
awkward at best.
Especially if it's you
who's secretly undressed.

Careless whispers cause
damage and harm.
Difficult to dispute.
Impossible to disarm.

If something can't be said
for all, loud and clear –
save conversation for later
when the coast is clear.

Maybe

It's possible.
There's hope.
Social synapse,
perhaps.

Fingers crossed.
We'll see.
Feasible.
Conceivable.

Strong maybe
doesn't mean
a positive *"yes"*.
Though it may suggest.

Nor does it mean *"no"*.
Ambivalent response
polishing uncertainty
for greater expectancy.

Can't say for sure if it's true.
All one can do is wait and see
if there's substance in the *"maybe"*
when action calls it due.

Imagination

For me,
imagination begins
before an idea.
Portal I peer in
to search
for solution.

Land of
infinite possibilities.
Unconventional
invention.
Waiting for
right moment to emerge.

Different twist.
Inspiration beyond
normalcy.
Where insight
and ingenuity
grow like flowers.

Flight of fantasy.
Imagination
allows me to
follow a path
many others
cannot see.

They are
stifled by the
mental and
physical restrictions
of the
"real" world.

Imagination
unburdens
and frees me from
such constraints.
Gives me vision.
Resourcefulness.

If I lost my way to
imagination,
all would seem
so damn ordinary.
I pray to continue to visit
anytime I desire.

Tightrope

Step carefully on the tightrope.
There's no fooling around.
Concentration. Balance.
Or you'll fall to the ground.

High, up in the sky,
let not your fate be fatal.
Focus on the finish line.
Pray the wire stable.

We walk the metaphor –
tightrope in our minds.
Critical, crucial challenge.
Tough and difficult bind.

To face it takes bravery.
Personal effort portrayed.
Courage to deal with obstacles.
Resolute and unafraid.

Another valiant effort.
Fortitude you expend.
But to fail won't mean a fall.
You can always try again.

Think of the highwire hero
living on to another day.
Allow it to be inspiration for
troubles that come your way.

Wicked Queen

Breathtaking.
Cut my oxygen
when nurse
left the room.

Intoxicating.
She slipped
me a Mickey.
Wanted Minnie.

Ambiguity.
Wondering
if I'm coming
or going.

Mesmerizing.
Baffled by
her vivacity
for scorn.

Exhilarating.
Paradox of
euphoria
and wrath.

Hostility.
Her grave and
somber bleakness.
Ferocity flourished.

Hilarity.
Dark humor.
Merriment at
my expense.

Tranquility.
Cherished,
treasured moments
when she's banished.

Horns of a Dilemma

Puzzling predicament.
Intangible impasse.
Catch 22 –
no matter what you do.

Difficult decision.
Fork in the road.
Perplexing plight.
One wrong. One right.

Horns of a dilemma.
Rock and a hard place.
Between devil and sea.
Face it. Decide. Or flee.

Lesser of two evils.
Least unpleasant
of both choices.
Resolution rejoices!

For every path chosen,
another's abandoned.
Move forward, head and heart.
Always a good place to start.

Three Wishes

Genie gave me three.
Three wishes to make life
what I would wish it to be.
With thought. Introspection.
Deliberation. Ample consideration.

Will I wish
for end of world hunger
or peace among nations?
Bring all religions in the world
under one denomination?

Or should I wish
for riches beyond
what's ever been known?
Servants for every whim.
King sitting at his throne.

I wish I could come up
with the right decisions.
Not allow opportunity to pass by.
Alas, my suppositions sealed my fate –
now with only two wishes to try.

I wish to make the most
of the time I have left.
Make my impact positive.
My approach, quite deft.
My story picturesque.

I wish there's a heaven
where I live beyond my death.
Understanding of the universe.
Surrounded by loved ones
with my purpose professed.

Beating a Dead Horse

Too many times
we attempt the futile –
good intentions
often brutal.

It's the human part
of our loving heart
to try, only to end
before it starts.

Not in our nature
to accept defeat.
We give it a whirl with
conscience's conceit.

Then comes realization.
Wisdom steps in.
Pointless. No purpose.
No use to begin.

When feat is fruitless –
there's no remorse.
Only desperate deniers
beat a dead horse.

Train yourself to listen to that small voice
that tells us what's important and what's not.
– Sue Grafton

Jiminy Cricket's Whisper

When I think of that
small voice in my brain –
Jiminy Cricket's whisper,
fully ingrained.

In *Pinocchio*, Jiminy is
careful common sense –
integrity, truthfulness,
beacon of balance.

Filter for every whim,
feeling or notion.
Redemption for my
human emotions.

Learned to listen
to Jiminy's concerns.
Watch out for trouble
or chance of being burned.

Early warning device
that sets off an alarm.
Whispers that keep me
from the ways of harm.

Pleasure Island dangers.
Donkey fever, alas.
His inside voice keeps me
from being a total ass.

In a Wonderland they lie,
Dreaming as the days go by,
Dreaming as the summers die:
Ever drifting down the stream –
Lingering in the golden dream –
Life, what is it but a dream?
  – Lewis Carrol

Life is but a Dream

We all have dreams when
we sleep, but may
not be as they seem –
if living life is truly but a dream.

In a way, we at least
direct the dream
we live within.
Real or not is how it spins.

Does it mean dreams
make life an illusion?
Living the dream –
with something more unseen?

Perhaps there lies another world
when dreams fully woken.
Beyond mortal comprehension –
another layer of ascension.

Reality beyond reality.
Behind the curtain we can't see.
Dreaming our myths and make believe.
Denying possibilities to perceive.

We collectively row our boats
gently down the stream.
Allowing nothing to intervene.
Accepting dreams as life serene.

"If you tell the truth, you don't have to remember anything."
– Mark Twain

Deception Pass

One thing worse
than getting caught
in a lie is the fear of
getting caught in a lie.

Once the lie is revealed,
it's a simple matter –
either own up to it
or invent another.

What's far worse is the
fear of being found out.
Constantly covering
one's tracks, 24/7.

Try to remember
the color painted
last time and match it
so no one notices.

Trouble being,
each lie to each person
comes in a different shade
with contradicting details.

Mark Twain was right.
Truth has no fear.
It's uncomplicated.
Requires no rehearsal.

Fear of being busted
completely disappears.
Nothing distorted
or embellished.

Truth, it turns out,
eliminates the fear
of fabrication.
There's no lie to hide.

Guideline

Conspire
to inspire.
Refuse the
superficial.
Talk the talk.
Walk the walk.
Lead to motivate –
beneficial.

Welcome
the spectrum.
Permanent
and temporary.
Many choices.
Many voices.
Thoughtful
sanctuary.

Produce.
Induce.
Song of
the solution.
Strong commit.
Gently submit.
Part of
our evolution.

Recognize
those in disguise.
Ambiguous
and vague.
Find distance
from resistance.
Compassionate
crusade.

Value of Nothing

Dylan once said,
"When you got nothing
you got nothing to lose."
But it's more than that.
We all begin as nothing
and turn it into something.

Nothing is a starting point.
The numeral zero.
It's not an absence,
but an entity entirely its own.
Cup waiting to be filled.
Space between the stars.

Nothing
is important.
It exists to be a measure.
Unoccupied expanse
keeping everything from
piling up on each other.

When there's no money
in the bank account.
Or a thought disappears
from your mind.
Nothing is something.
Nothing has value.

Ozzie and Harriet

In the late 1950's
and early 60's
television portrayal
of American life
more delusion
than illusion.

Scripts had next
to nothing about
activism, equality
or civil rights.
Segregation. Racism.
Fantasy Americanism.

In fairness, these shows
meant to entertain,
not educate or inform.
They were anything but
"the good old days."
Reality purposely erased.

Some might wish we could
go back in time when
women were housewives
and husbands would
bring home ice cream.
Life seemed so serene.

Bias. Fairyland
in the first place.
How would the real Ozzie
confront the black family
who moved in next door?
Protest? Go to court?

Harriet arrested marching in
a non-violent demonstration.
Ricky with a drug problem.
David's really gay.
Ozzie comes up with a plan
helped by buddies in the Ku Klux Klan.

Might be a different world
if television had the courage
to show the way it was.
But remember, dear viewers,
no one knew what Ozzie did.
Perhaps his job was sordid!

Airplane Window

Inside this metal bird,
I peer out at the runway –
watch myself soar into sky
and depart earthen world.

I'm always amazed
at the mass of
uninhabited land
still anticipating civilization.

Snowcapped mountain peaks.
Arid deserts and green valleys.
Lakes like puddles.
Rivers, just a slither.

When communities are apparent,
I'm reminded of matchbox cars
and miniature playhouses seen
from a ten story view.

It all looks so surreal.
Then I realize that it is me
who is surreal, miles high,
going 500 miles an hour.

Plane flies across rooftops,
opens flaps, lowers wheels –
routine touch down for
a perfect landing.

Taxi to destination's gate.
Workers unload baggage.
I leave the window behind.
See the world from the ground.

Louder than Words

It's not what we say,
but what we do.
Action, the traction,
that make a promise true.

Talk can sprout wings
and simply flutter away.
Actual effort, an exert,
to move ahead today.

Some speak in emptiness –
words that have no soul.
Believed, then deceived,
when there's nothing to behold.

Movement beyond the blarney.
Past the wall of good intention.
Faction for satisfaction –
do it without mention.

Actions do speak louder
than any verbal vow.
Roaring and resounding –
deafens saying it aloud.

Modern Café

Drink from the cup
of contemporary.
Reconcile
to be in style.

Abandon past –
obsolete, outdated,
antiquated, passé.
Fossils from another day.

Metaphysical place
in your mind.
Noxious and rotten
past, all but forgotten.

New items
on the menu.
Sure to impress.
Futuristic. Fresh.

A place to toast today –
leave bygones behind.
Avant-garde,
the vanguard.

I enjoy going there
to get a taste of new.
But not the only diner
where the fare is finer.

I still visit old haunts.
Comfort food as a meal.
Memories served as a filet –
The Old-Fashioned Vintage Café.

Unwritten Rule

Hug from farmer's daughter
certainly brightened my day.
Her childlike innocence
openly ready to play.

Unable to control myself
I took the fatal step.
One and one together
up in the hayloft we *"slept."*

It did not extend my bliss –
in fact, it scorched my path.
Wrathful host in anger
well aware of my carnal gaffe.

Broke the unwritten rule –
Don't sleep where you eat.
Said we should get married.
Shotgun pointed at my seat.

No matter the energetic ecstasy –
it's more important to survive.
Changed my life completely
but at least I'm still alive.

Expectations

On one hand,
an expectation
is a standard measure –
allowing an experience
to be above or below
what we thought it would be.

It also delivers
delight or disappointment
based upon preconceived thought.
It's subconscious purpose
is a shelter of protection
from the unknown.

What if there were no expectations?
Every situation happening
as it is supposed to,
without comparison or analysis.
Would we cultivate a more truthful
solution to personal interaction?

Would it
enhance the experience?
Simply enjoy everything
as it is without
personal parameters?
Let it all shine without scrutiny?

It would be a challenge.
Certainly, something to ponder.
To be in the moment without
all the baggage of restrictions.
Being bare to the
reality of the world.

Eight Days a Week

What if we suddenly had
an extra day to play?
Eight instead of seven.
Another day
to while away
at our own discretion.

Three day weekend,
mandatory requisite.
Twenty-four hours more
for our benefit.
1440 minutes
to live within it.

Never enough time
to get everything done.
Extra moments –
better than none.
More to cram in
to see what becomes.

More time.
Wonderful gift.
Totally unexpected
phenomenal shift.
Use or procrastinate?
Choice still persists.

Alas, we're limited
to a week with seven.
Sunday through Saturday –
days in succession.
Can't squeeze another day in.
But it's fun to imagine.

"Be a bush if you can't be a tree. If you can't be a highway,
just be a trail. If you can't be a sun, be a star. For it isn't by size
that you win or fail. Be the best of whatever you are."
– Martin Luther King

Your Best Self

Good advice, really.
Be the best that you can be.
Show your true self.
Top of your game.

For some,
that's not good enough.
They pretend to be
another character altogether.

Customized to fit
the clueless audience.
Hoping for greater
appreciation and respect.

The façade
gives an impression
of one person, but
dismisses another.

Unfortunately,
the individual
banished is
the real one.

How sad it is to
require a mask to
feel good enough
to be accepted.

Reveal who you are.
Let the chips fall
where they may.
Truth is a virtue.

Then, there's no worry
of using the wrong role
or false pretenses. Be real.
Authenticity attracts like a magnet.

Aspiration

Dream.
Acquire ambition.
Desire. Passion.
Yearn for a
better tomorrow.

Seek ways
to strive.
Pursue your heart.
Long for ideals
not in your grasp.

Be not content
with status quo.
Accomplishment
happens only
through growth.

Allow aspiration
to blaze new trails.
Shepherd amazement.
Keep moving
the goalposts ahead.

Aspire for
authenticity.
Anticipate
adventure.
Awaken to awe.

Pack Rat

There he sat.
With time to chat.
Chance to spat.
No cattle, all hat.
Sanitation scat.
Boiled a big vat.
Technique down pat.
Attracted gnats –
belfry with bats.
Plethora of cats.
Tit for tat –
this for that.
Knows where nothing's at.
Collects doormats.
Deal-making diplomat.
Tidiness falls flat.
Bohemian brat.

Pack rat.

Angel Food

As a kid, I was given a choice of cake
to be baked for my birthday.
It was always angel food cake.
Obviously. White. Fluffy. Light.
And to top it off,
it's the food of angels!

My younger sister, on the other hand,
would insist on devil's food.
Not only because she liked to be different
but the dense, dark, rich, fudgy cake
was her absolute favorite.
I, of course, teased her mercilessly.

In my childlike mind, any association
with angels elevated my standing
to a more blessed and holy place.
When I blew out the candles I knew
they were looking down upon me
with heavenly approval.

I did have a slither of concern
that my dear sister was
going down a precarious path
with the Prince of Darkness.
Every year, she'd hold hands with Satan
and request the delicious demon dessert.

Though I found her selection tasty
I couldn't take the risk myself.
With an overactive imagination,
one can never be too careful
to avoid tipping the scales from
entering the pearly gates to the door of hell.

"Angel food cake, please,"
said the boy with the halo.

*Isn't it good after an airplane trip to go home
and look at some peaches on a plate?*
– Francis Ponge

Homeward Resound

I believe in the importance of travel.
Flying the friendly skies.
Enjoying the desired destination.
Getting away from it all.

But being a jetsetter today
is a long cry from the
classy and elegant
experience of the past.

Schedule delays.
Cancellations. Overbooking.
Fighting the onerous current
against a sea of humanity.

Now it's like riding a bus.
Except, bus seats are
likely a lot more comfortable
with more elbow room.

When the trip is over
there's nothing like the
warm hearted comfort
of coming home.

The reassurance of familiar.
Be it peaches on a plate,
a hug from a loved one
or friendly purr from a pet.

In your own place.
In your own bed.
Your everyday routine.
With no set check-out time.

One Hundred Years Ago

Price of bread was twelve cents.
Average annual wage – $1,254.
Life expectancy less than 60.
Prohibition helped many *"speak-easy."*
Radio, the rage, playing
"Yes, We Have No Bananas."
King Tut's tomb discovered.
First helicopter flew.
Hitler failed a coup.

It was my grandparent's reality.
Just as hard to
look back and understand
as it would be
for them to imagine us now.
I wonder which group
most adaptable if a
time machine sent us back
and transported them to today.

It's an interesting exercise.
We might adapt to the old ways
but probably wouldn't like it.
Miss all the technology that
hadn't been invented yet.
Brain/encyclopedia/camera/phone
no longer in one's pocket to
pull out in a moment's notice
and answer/research/document/call.

On the other hand, future travelers
would likely be averse to
comprehending and learning
all the incredible new things
available at their fingertips.
They'd still drink in bars.
Write letters with pen in script.
Cook a pot roast for Sunday dinner.
Unburdened by new technology.

Through Our Eyes

When young
we admire our parents.
Believe what they believe.
See their silhouettes
through our eyes.

As we get older,
our eyes begin to
see differently,
no matter the allegiance.
Our own epiphanies.

Not nefarious, but natural.
We grow into ourselves
thanks to their beloved guidance.
There should be no contempt
for a different point of view.

Yet, sometimes there
is hostility. Scorn.
How could the fruit
of their loins believe
such incendiary ideology?

It is a passage of life.
When parents realize
their sun-drenched skies
are seen as cloudy
through our eyes.

Maybe we observe
contempt they cannot.
Towering truths
upon our tranquility.
Our view. Our eyes. Our life.

"Like sands through the hourglass, so are the days of our lives."
– Opening intro to the soap opera, ***Days of Our Lives***

Where Does the Time Go?

For many years, I never really
thought about retirement.
Nose to the grindstone.
Full steam ahead.

I imagined the luxury of
enormous time on my hands.
All the hours a week I worked
would then be free time.

Part of me wondered how
such a void could be filled.
Now that retirement arrived,
the question's answered.

It's a retirement fantasy to believe
there would be a large hole to fill.
Like in water, footsteps disappear
the minute you take another.

Sand in the hourglass travels
much faster than before.
Minutes fly by
rather than meander.

Instead of time on my hands,
it escaped from its cage and
took flight toward the heavens.
Moments, more precious, remain.

My day is as full as it was
when I worked sixty hours a week.
Worrying about fitting in
all the things I want to do.

Where does the time go?
It changes. Morphs. Transforms.
Into accelerated days, weeks, years.
Retirement just tries to catch up.

Leavenworth Birthday

It was a time
when we were more
footloose and fancy free.
Donna and I settled into
Sleeping Lady Mountain Resort
200 miles away from home
to celebrate my birthday.

A text on my phone from
two hometown friends
simply said
"We're coming to share your day."
Didn't say when. Or how.
I was quite surprised.
Felt honored. Loved.

By afternoon, they had
a place to stay in town
and drove out to see us.
Found a lovely restaurant
for dinner where they
presented an expensive
20-year bottle of wine.

An unexpected evening –
full of good food, laughter and
conversation that can only
come from real friendship.
Midnight at the resort pool –
swimming under the stars.
How I valued that day.

When I think of the numerous
good times we shared together,
that birthday was a highlight.
Friendships do fade, unfortunately.
When we moved 150 miles away
to Walla Walla –
crickets.

I know that the term
"out of sight, out of mind"
can be a real thing.
Perhaps it's because of
not seeing each other
on a regular basis anymore.
It was quick, like a light switch.

People get busy.
Guess I'm old fashioned,
but I don't believe friendships
should disintegrate and disappear
because of a three hour drive.
Great friendships endure
no matter time or distance.

SIX years since we made
the move to wine country.
Many things here we'd
love to share with those friends.
To relive that special day
in Leavenworth –
this time in Walla Walla.

One cannot push a string.
It may be time to abandon
what I would like to happen
and except the inevitable.
Realize the magic we had in
Leavenworth won't reoccur.
Sleeping Lady still slumbers.

Bear With Me

There he sits
torn and tattered
waiting for his
next little human
to come along
and be his friend.

He's had quite a few.
First, he's embraced.
Bedtime companion.
Tea party partaker.
Secret holder –
sworn to silence.

Trouble with humans
is that they grow up.
After a few years,
his person has
better things to do
than pretend.

Relegated to the
dark confines
of the toy box.
Eventually
tossed out
or given away.

He knows it's not over.
Some young heart
will find its way to him –
have Mom sew some tears
and he'll be the best of bears
until he's again outgrown.

That's the trouble
stuck in time without end.
The world continues
to adapt and change
when you can't –
but can only grin and bear it.

Teddy

His last name was Bear,
but it was rarely used.
Teddy was my friend.
Playmate. Companion.
First cuddle in the
morning and last
before sleep at night.

Teddy. Plush and furry.
Good listener.
Willing participant
for any and all
imaginative adventures.
Picnics. Flashlight tag.
Cops & Robbers. Hide n' seek.

Teddy was someone
to hear all my secrets.
Promised never to tell
another soul. Pinky swear.
Trusted Teddy
beyond anyone – more
than mom and dad.

Sentimental celebration
of one of life's times
when imagination
more real than reality.
Getting older, growing up,
seeing the world without
Teddy regrettably happens.

If those memories can be
revived and remembered
decades later –
joy of innocence returns.
Teddy, secrets and all,
stops by for a cup of tea.
Reality's overrated.

To Mom

You were a great mom.
A little overprotective, but
that comes with the territory
of me being the first child.

I remember you referred to
the big green book on childcare
written by Dr. Benjamin Spock
on a nearly daily basis.

Although you were fragile
from a bout of rheumatic fever
in your teens, very few knew
of the weakened heart condition.

I was in second grade and you
were prescribed complete bedrest
to get over life-threatening pneumonia
which lasted many tough months.

After that, you built yourself back.
Bowling. Swimming. Tending a half acre garden.
Feeding chickens. Slopping hogs.
While raising me, my sister – and Dad.

You were tough. Determined. Smart.
Yet, kind and sympathetic for first aid
on numerous skinned knees and
accidental exposure to stinging nettles.

You glowed when I got married.
Celebrated your first grandchild.
A feeling I never totally understood
until I had one of my own.

You were always loving,
supportive and interested
in my work and latest creations.
It was always fun to share them.

You had so much talent as
a self-taught artist. I loved your
pine needle baskets, wood carvings –
especially all the original Santas.

That was the gift you
passed on to me – the ability
to tackle anything creatively and
offer my own personal solution.

After a painful decline, you succumbed
to congestive heart failure in 2013.
You're still with me in my heart
with thousands of mother memories.

Thank you for being my mom.
I may not have been the easiest
to raise, but you were always
up for the challenge. I'm living proof.

Leaving Home

Never asked permission
when it came to leaving.
One summer, told parents
I was staying near college
and not coming home
three hundred miles away.

My father was a difficult read.
Shrugged his shoulders –
went for another cup of coffee.
Mother's smiling face
fell instantly into dejection.
Dismally despondent.

On one hand, I felt horrible
causing such sadness.
Had she not prepared herself
for the obvious inevitable?
Or was it one more summer
to steal with me?

Such are the tribulations
coming of age.
I was ready for independence.
Eager to start on my own.
A mother's apron strings
pull hard at a son's heart.

Being oldest, it was the first time
parents watched their sparrow
fly from nest into the unknown.
All the worries and concerns
about my circumstance and outcome
bundled into that particular moment.

An unscheduled surgery.
Leaving home meant saying so long
to the family norm since birth.
A melancholy goodbye,
but a *hello* to new horizons.
A son ready to face the world.

Green, My Healing Color

Green awakens again
from its winter slumber.
Still sleepy-eyed,
it starts slow and sluggish
like before morning coffee
kicks in.

Yellow lawns begin
to get their color back
one blade of grass at a time.
Leaves emerge from
small brown buds
spawning glorious shade.

But it's the feeling of green
I love the most.
The freshness.
The calmness.
The color of life
peacefully making me feel alive.

Just as green
symbolizes rebirth,
it heals my heart
and soothes my soul.
Repairing my broken branches –
rejuvenating my growth.

Red Velvet Footstool

After grandmother passed
it was all I wanted from her home.
An upholstered soft mohair
red velvet footstool padded
with childhood memories.

I remember being small enough
to curl up and lie on it like a bed.
Listening to my grandparents
talking softly to each other –
black & white Zenith flickering.

I realized I didn't need anything more
to remind me of the memories
the little footstool contained.
Fragrance of Half & Half pipe tobacco
among her purple African violets.

When I see the footstool now
I'm transported back in time.
Enjoying the same
wooden alphabet blocks
my father played with.

Remembering when I was little
and everything else so big.
A warm, comfy piece of furniture –
just the right size that fit
my childhood world perfectly.

Whisper Come Hither

Under your breath –
a whisper.
Couldn't quite hear it.
Auditory blister.

Not to be dramatic or
make an enormous huff.
A bit abnormal when communication
is usually up to snuff.

Perhaps ears are failing
and meant for me to hear.
Long abandoned argument?
Something more severe?

Would it leave emotional scar?
Impinge upon my confidence?
Humiliate my sense of self
completely without defense?

Whispering out of range.
A yawn would be more telling.
Am I too self-absorbed to
believe it was compelling?

Just a guess at this point.
Pretend it didn't happen.
Haunting words I almost knew –
simply a distraction.

Banana Man

I try to eat
a banana
every day.

Give my body
potassium
the easy way.

Don't like
ripe mushy
bananas to eat.

Too soft.
Too stringy.
Too overly sweet.

Prefer some green
on the yellow.
I'm picky.

Makes
shopping for
bananas tricky.

Find one
almost perfect
for the next day.

The rest greener –
ripen over time
and still be ok.

Delicate balance –
find the correct
combination.

Sometimes it
doesn't work out –
overly ripe abomination.

I choke it down
and head to the
store for more.

Buying bananas
drives me bananas
before I'm done.

But morning breakfast
wouldn't be the
same without one.

Sadie Hawkins Dance

Switched social norm –
this time, girl asks boy.
Dress like a hillbilly
with corncob pipe
and be the real McCoy.

Went as a scarecrow.
She as Daisy Mae.
Cuddling carriage ride
to the festivities.
Photo with bales of hay.

Hoofin' at the hoedown.
Promenade as a pair.
Caller starts the do-si-do –
sidestep to apple cider.
Shooting stars in the air.

Cozy warmth of fireplace.
Steaming mugs in hand.
She made the first move
with sweet hug and kiss –
and I, under her command.

Dying embers can still start a fire
– Chinese Proverb

Dying Embers

As I get older,
the hot embers of youth
fade and glow less than before.

With age come wisdom,
tempering previous
flash in the pan impulsiveness.

Physically, I feel the
embers withering –
tuckering out too early.

The one thing to
never forget is
I can still make fire.

Might take extra blowing,
kindling and care –
but there's fire under there.

Which means
no matter the birthdays,
I still make a difference.

I will not
give up the good fight or
acquiesce my God given rights.

The older generation
may appear harmless.
Dying embers, after all.

Igniting interest,
flames to inferno –
my spark will rage on.

"The poetry of the earth is never dead."
– John Keats

Fred

Today, Fred the turkey
paid us a visit again –
all puffed up in
amazing feather regalia,
pompously preening
at his reflected image in
our sliding glass doors.

While all the other turkeys
who came for cracked corn
during the winter have gone,
to find new mates and
fresh stomping grounds,
Fred is content to hang alone
to our confusion and amusement.

He is a poem about loneliness.
Finding solace in the familiar.
Visiting his other friends:
the red-winged blackbirds,
doves, quail and squirrels –
still feeding on sunflower seeds
provided daily in the feeders.

Marches to a different drummer.
Declares our place his home base
even though other brethren
have seasonally departed.
Nature not only provides
poetry for instinctual ones,
there are anomalies like Fred.

There's beauty in earth's vast
garden of plants and animals.
A poem, each unto themselves.
Not all poems are symmetrical
or rhyme at the right time.
Predictability is so boring.
Instead, a poem in Fred.

Kiss Me

"Kiss Me," said the frog,
"I will turn into a handsome prince."

Takes faith to believe
in a talking magic frog.
Especially one
in a swampy bog.

Not the first time he asked –
certainly not the last.
No fulfillment of a kiss had
happened in the past.

Tried talking about
his fame and fortune,
but the future wasn't creating
female fervor any time soon.

To him, it was futility.
Frustration then set in.
Feared a kiss would never come.
Failure set to win.

Decided to focus
on just being a frog.
Have fun with the freedom.
Clear his feelings from fog.

It was then a friendship
happened to occur.
She took a walk and found him.
Her kiss removed the curse.

Whether folly or fantasy
one thing does ring true.
Finding yourself is essential
when love is overdue.

"When you fish for love, bait with your heart, not your brain."
– Mark Twain

Fishing for Love

Full tackle box.
Plenty of lures.
But wait...
they're biting now
on love as bait.

Get out #10 hook.
Tie with 4lb. leader.
Add a light weight.
Cast out with compassion.
Watch line become straight.

Patience a virtue.
Never know when.
Tug at the heart.
Pull up and hook it.
Play it, careful and smart.

Start reelin'.
Navigate net.
See what's caught.
Hoist in the boat.
A Cuddlefish it's not!

Fishing for love
less a sport
than inclination.
Even with good bait –
still might be infatuation.

Tip of the Iceberg

*Ninety percent of an iceberg
is hidden under the surface.*

We only see a
portion of a person.
Makes us think we
know more than we do.

There's always a lot
underneath that
remains hidden.
More than imagined.

Emotional scars.
Addictions.
Bad habits.
Eccentricities.

Unapparent.
Sleight of hand.
Intentional diversion.
Deliberately disguised.

Lurking
below the surface
in deep, cold water
slumbering.

Until it
runs aground.
More surface exposed –
alters our perception.

Some icebergs
larger than others.
Some tips
more deceptive.

It's not what you know.
It's what you don't know.
What you don't see
is the perilous pariah.

Knowing someone
deep down
is the only way
to escape the danger.

Fireworks

That's the way it begins –
Emotional fireworks. Starry-eyed.
Enchantment. Spellbinding.
Lovers' yearning. Euphoria.
Harmonious infatuation.

The honeymoon phase.
Intense intimacy explored.
Both head and heart
enraptured in both passion
and dreamy devotion.

Initially emotionally explosive –
feelings of affection warp into
unwavering romance and closeness.
Mutual allure. Amiable adoration.
Committed, connected relationship.

Eventually, fireworks fade.
In its place, something even better
manifests into joyful, serene love.
Transcendent treasure.
Tenderness and truth.

As the grand finale ends,
stars still light the skies –
sparks continue to provide
sentimental serenity, blissful bonding –
where balance and gentleness prevail.

*Sometimes all a person needs is a hand to hold
and a heart to understand.*
– Andy Rooney

Loving Touch

When you care,
it's easy to share.
When one's defeated,
nurture when needed.

You can be the ear
to listen to their fear.
Shoulder there to lean
when life's not serene.

Be the hand to hold
as emotions unfold.
Heart of compassion –
most appropriate action.

We need each other
to help discover
how to heal
the sadness we feel.

Hug and embrace –
never replaced.
Gentle words spoken
for someone broken.

Fragile

Something you should know.
Something I must share.
When it comes to my open heart –
please, handle with care.

Strength of stability.
Steady, never falter.
Stand by, thick or thin.
Solid Rock of Gibraltar.

Swear upon my mother's grave –
be the gallant white knight.
Bend instead of break.
Stand for what is right.

Love for me is fragile.
Delicate flower preserved.
In contrast to my fortitude –
my achilles when it's spurred.

Let's continue this enchanted life.
Not allow love to fade.
Protect precious connection.
Heroes of our light brigade.

Magic Carpet Ride

Come ride on my magic carpet.
Let's fly the friendly skies.
You, me and this Turkish rug –
sorcery makes it rise.

Hovering over rooftops.
Soaring over trees.
Why walk when we can
take flight with such ease?

True, we must dress for weather.
Hold on tight for gusts of wind.
Takes us where we wish –
and places never imagined.

Magic carpets find locations
with no latitude or longitude.
Oasis. Hidden valley. Secret cave.
High adventure in magnitude.

Powered by imagination –
no limit where we go.
Moon and Mars a wish away –
beyond the things we know.

Join my magic carpet ride.
Experience the journey together.
Explorations, odysseys and passages
that we will share, forever.

Spirit Whisper

Comes out of nowhere.
Not spoken but
still understood.
Spirit Whisper.

Guide for indecision.
Directs the correct path.
Beacon of clarity.
Hidden helping hand.

Inner voice verbalizes
to you alone.
Wrestles with previous
thoughts and actions.

Advice, nonetheless.
Taken to heart or not.
Signpost assistance
to ignore if you want.

Spirit Whisper.
There when you need it.
A shove in the right direction.
But only if you heed it.

To get the full value of joy you must have someone to divide it with."
– Mark Twain

Joy ^{2}

How grateful I am
to share the
joy of life
with someone.

Sharing
smiles, tears,
hopes, fears,
grief and fun.

Good, bad
happy and sad.
Hand in hand –
all we face together.

Lean upon
each other.
Being there
whenever.

A kiss is
only a motion
when blown
into the wind.

When received
by another,
it's emotion
unimagined.

True, there
can be joy –
solo and
on one's own.

Joy squared
exponentially better
when one
is not alone.

Hocus Pocus

Wish of a
magic wand –
wave my troubles
far beyond.

Quiet the noise
with a little spell.
Stop the screams.
Send devil to hell.

Create potion so
justice prevails.
Wizard's wrath.
Evil fails.

Pins in place.
Vengeance style.
Voodoo due.
Vanish the vile.

Hocus Pocus.
Abracadabra.
Incantation invokes
bewitched bonanza.

If only that easy
to stop my distress.
Rid life of all
the wickedness.

Such rituals only
apparitions in real life.
Phantom ghosts can't
kill with a knife.

Above all, don't lie to yourself.
– Fyodor Dostoevsky

Authenticity

If you don't feel
the way they say
you're supposed to feel,
it's ok.
Feel *your* way.

If you don't think
the way they say
you're supposed to think,
it's ok.
Think *your* way.

If you don't act
the way they say
you're supposed to act,
it's ok.
Act *your* way.

If you don't love
the way they say
you're supposed to love,
it's ok.
Love *your* way.

Your reflection,
the only emulation.
Don't succumb
to expectations
or manipulations.

You can pretend
if you must –
just to fit in.
Don't forget what's real –
under the mask, genuine.

Empathy

Give away jealousy.
Add a cup of respect.
Bake a cake of compassion.
Serve with a sweet connect.

Put yourself in another's place
See the world through new eyes.
Admire strength, perseverance.
Forgiveness without sacrifice.

With more kindheartedness
discover a healthier game.
Far better than attacking
anything strange.

Like a rainbow promise
for a more harmonious time –
Empathy, the missing candle
to light the cliff to climb.

Once in a Blue Moon

It happens, but not often.
Two souls realize their swoon –
share a rare connection
scarce as a blue moon.

A relationship
few and far between.
Out of the ordinary.
Love in purest extreme.

Nothing comes easy.
Takes work to make it work.
Kindness and affection
helps disagreements convert.

Some people are envious.
Wish it had happened to them.
Spoiling such happiness with
words and actions that condemn.

It's difficult to destroy this
extraordinary precious gift.
The bond of the blue moon
helps the couple persist.

They persevere and prevail
despite detours and roadblocks.
Combination to contentment –
there for them to unlock.

Colors of My Within

Color me red.
Human heart.
Passionate fire.
Unwavering love.

Color me blue.
Robin egg iris.
Denim dependable.
True blue.

Color me yellow.
Sunny smile.
Buttercup bouquet.
Golden rule.

Color me green.
Budding ideas.
Emerald ethics.
Tender turf.

Color me purple.
Amethyst attitude.
Violet vibes.
Plum crazy.

Magic Binoculars

Pair of magic binoculars
looks beyond the horizon,
peers past the physical realm –
observes the future.

The lens reveals
forthcoming events,
imminent disasters
and impending doom.

What about kindness?
Why so difficult to observe
good in the world when
the stage is set by bad?

Is it because we look for it?
Love works silently
without pandemonium,
bluster and hullabaloo.

It's not sensational.
No bombs, no flames,
no anger or hate.
Much good is invisible.

Binoculars see in distance
conflagration – an inferno.
Fear eyes focus on
worst case scenario.

Flames blind us from
examining what really matters.
If our binoculars could only see
the wonder instead.

The L Word

Four letter word
finally said –
from the heart,
not the head.

Such a risk,
this unveil.
Is it real or
fairytale?

Emotion shared
by another's lips?
Or one-sided
relationship?

Can't come undone.
Soul emancipate.
Was it too soon
or far too late?

Takes courage.
Bravery. Daring.
Genie out of bottle.
Affectionate airing.

Feelings revealed.
Devotion's desire.
Gift without wrapping.
Amore aspired.

L word emerges.
No longer restrained.
Let loose into the wild.
Unknown terrain.

Fine Wine, Aged

Some wines get
better with age.
More complex aromas.
More depth to the taste.
Robust, complex flavors.
Smoother, silkier.
Less astringent.

We burst onto the scene
like a young wine –
Spicy. Juicy.
Luscious primary flavors,
fresh and crisp.
As we age, I believe
love gets better, too.

Time has turned our love
into a well-aged wine.
Revealing full complexity
with nuanced, earthy flavors.
Resonant developed character.
Softer, more mellow,
making color deeper together.

I now sip from our love and
appreciate the years in the barrel.
Boldness softens to gentleness,
enhancing the mature bouquet.
Letting sediment, not sentiment
fall to the bottom.
Savoring our structure and stability.

Nothing's Perfect

She said it was
one of those things.
Take the grim
as well as the good.
Part of the deal
with anything real –
it should be understood.

My naivete taken back.
Something never considered.
Silver lining has a cloud.
Rose – prickly thorns.
Take completely whole
as it comes into the fold.
Accept all without scorn.

Every sword, a double edge.
All that glitters isn't gold.
The best cloth may have a moth.
Bones come with the meat.
Nothing perfect, peerless or pure.
But it's something we must endure.
Even chocolate – bittersweet.

Hourglass

After midnight countdown,
hourglass begins anew.
Sand sifts another year
till December bids adieu.

Every year, a reset.
Listen better, love more,
laugh longer, live refreshed.
Care and compassion soar.

New friends. Add memories.
Read. Relax. Play. Create.
Time stops for no one.
It doesn't pay to wait.

Hourglass, a reminder.
Moments passing by.
Make the most of it all –
or at least an honest try.

Resolutions for the New Year

New year. New beginning.
Good time for change.
Turn bad habits into good.
Priorities to rearrange.

Lose weight – quite popular.
Drink less, exercise more.
Eat healthier. Better food.
Stop slamming the door.

No matter what our intentions,
each year the list is the same.
Wants. Dreams. Desires.
All tend to go down the drain.

It's one thing to make a list.
Another for it to come true.
Total optimism at the onset.
Abandoning routine – hard to do.

Changes we attempt to make –
lost after a month or two.
The challenge not realized is the
metamorphosis aimed at you.

It's not habits we must change
but ourselves to make it real.
Adamant. Permanent. Resolute.
Will always seal the deal.

Onward

January begins as baby –
grows to elder
by December's end.
By then, no spring chicken.
Tired. Exhausted. Drained.
Bone weary. Worn out.

At the beginning once more.
Fresh start. Optimistic.
New eyes at the world.
Different mindset.
Anticipation for all
what's in store.

It's a New Year.
Flame again anew –
not sputtering at the wick.
Time of renewal.
Another year of hope
added to the warranty.

Chalk one more up.
Turn over hourglass
for another go at it.
Encore with new song.
Perhaps better than
just a repeat performance.

Past – full of memories
that can't be altered –
only forgotten.
Future – forged in real time.
New clean slate.
Plethora of possibilities.

Off the starting blocks,
let the marathon commence.
On your mark. Get set. *Go!*
Race at your own pace.
Your competition is only
the person you were before.

Gift of the Month

Never been the
lucky recipient
of a generous
gift-of-the-month.

Anticipating
twelve surprises
throughout the year.
Not in one big lump.

Let January be jam.
Perfect present of preserves.
February follows with fudge
which I will not begrudge.

March, exotic mandarins.
Easy to peel and eat.
April, tasty almonds –
a healthy crunchy treat.

May, mulberry muffins –
full of baked goodness.
June, beef jerky.
Glad it isn't turkey.

July – hoped for pie cuisine,
but end up with jellybeans.
August, apricots.
Just a few, not a lot.

September, shellfish.
Not sharing would be selfish.
October, onions.
Walla Walla Sweets never shunned.

November, navy bean soup.
Lunch and laxative in one clean swoop.
December, darjeeling tea.
A fine way to remember me!

Gift of the month –
treats abound.
Presents give pleasure
all year around.

Curse the Groundhog

The worry of a little boy
seeing his shadow at recess.
He was so hoping for
a shorter winter, but now,
it would be six more cold weeks.

Teacher explained
about the groundhog –
scared by his shadow,
burrowing back into
his den hibernation.

It was obviously real.
A holiday, after all.
Somehow this rodent
could foretell the weather and
predict the ominous forecast.

The boy didn't question the
credentials of the creature.
Lack of metrological knowledge.
Or dubious reasoning of a
bad omen on a sunny day.

He only knew it meant
bundling up for chilly conditions
and spring coming much later
than he was hoping for.
More cool, frigid days ahead.

Groundhog, quite comfortable
in his warm underground lair.
While baseball takes a
back seat until flowers bloom.
Curse that pompous portender!

Cupid's Arrow

Aims not to maim.
Deadeye to desire.
Targets true love.
No Romeo required.

Clever little cherub.
Bow and quiver ready.
Arrow released from drawstring.
Shooting always steady.

Cannot dodge the arrow.
Nothing left to do –
helpless and moonstruck
toward your *dream come true*.

Once you've been hit,
you'll feel it in your heart.
Heartwarming with no warning.
Obsession from the start.

Then, the world is different.
Inexpressible amour.
Captive and committed.
Togetherness implored.

You can curse Cupid's arrow
or thank him just the same.
A deep, wonderful wound with
far more passion than pain.

"*March is a tomboy with tousled hair, a mischievous smile,
mud on her shoes, and a laugh in her voice.*"
– Hal Borland

Miss March

Such a tease, Miss March.
Maybe because spring
is just around the corner.
We wait for winter's end
with impatient hope.

Dissociative disorder.
Split personality.
She doesn't know
who she should be –
hour after hour, day after day.

Dainty, she is not.
Blustery, boisterous, brazenly
unpredictable behavior are
presumptions we must have
before we welcome her in.

Yet, invite her in, we do.
Year after year, hoping
for more docile demeanor.
Benevolent warmth.
Sunny disposition.

She laughs because
just a taste of radiance
perks up spirits enough
to open optimism.
Toy with our trust.

Then bashes tranquility
with wracked wretchedness –
wind, water and other
worrisome weather to
douse any delusion of delight.

A house guest we love
and hate at the same time.
If we weren't all related
it might be a different story.
At least we know what we're in for.

*"It was one of those March days when the sun shines hot
& the wind blows cold: when it is summer in the light
and winter in the shade."*
  – Charles Dickens

Dress Dilemma

Searing in the sun, shivering in the shade.
March, the most inconvenient month
to dress with proper attire, I'm afraid.

In the sun, the goal, stay cool.
Light colors and cotton let the body breathe.
Less is more, no sweat, that's the rule.

In the shade, avoid the shiver.
Bundle up and layer –
Dark colors and wool deliver.

What to do about March weather?
Hot and cold at the same time,
with no solution to handle it together.

Dress for the sun, avoid the shade.
Stay out of cold dark shadows –
Warm oneself and sunbathe.

If the sun disappears with an icy wind
and it all becomes the freezing shade,
simply go inside until it's nice again.

And you will have it made.

Arc of March

Comes in
a roaring lion.
Exits
a gentle lamb.

Still Winter.
Spring approaching.
Transition month
metamorphosis.

Kites greet the skies –
tease the windy breeze.
Daffodils and tulips emerge.
Color the garden scene.

Ides, midway upon us.
Leprechauns we acquiesce.
Shamrock luck, basketball madness,
where winners bask in success.

Arc of March – variation
greater than any other season.
More outdoors than in –
celebration on the horizon.

Rainy Day in April

I watch the rain fall –
inside, I'm warm and dry.
So cloudy, dark and wet –
good day to stay home and cry.

Water on the window –
prism for me to peer.
Seeing the world in sadness
when the view is less than clear.

People pass by hurriedly
dodging raindrops in the wind.
Avoiding puddles, in their haste,
they get wetter than imagined.

Patters on my pane
tell me the storm isn't over.
I am but its audience
ducking the exposure.

For me, the rain effects
my mood and sodden thoughts.
Gloomy, emotionally turbulent –
a day to be distraught.

Eventually, the rain will pass –
my window clear again.
Sunshine to lift my spirits.
Blue sky to heal lament.

But a rainy day in April
does what it's supposed to do.
Water for emerging buds
when downtime takes its queue.

"April hath put a spirit of youth in everything."
– William Shakespeare

April Blossoms

One of the reasons for
a move to Walla Walla
was the early visit of Spring.
Green lawns and leaves
reveal considerably sooner.
Tree blossoms
burst out in rapture.

I don't believe Spring
makes me feel younger
but the explosion of color –
influx of bird songs –
throaty croaks of frogs –
enhance my world and
puts a spring in my step.

April brings showers, true.
It also begins to melt the
white frosting on the foothills.
In the wildlife world,
it's a mating dance for all critters.
Time to grow, replenish, renew.
I love it when April blossoms.

Sign of Spring

Saw the first sign of Spring today.
An Orange Fluorescent Vested Flagger
with bright safety green plumage.
They appear after Winter,
gathering in numbers as
Spring segues into Summer.

One of the curious attributes
of these strange birds
is an appendage
attached to a large sign –
red on one side and
yellow on the other...

Many times, you can observe
them holding a device
up to the head, talking to it,
prior to rotating the sign color.
It's understood this is how
the unusual breed communicates.

To many automobile drivers,
this species is considered invasive
because of hindrance
to normal schedules and
unwanted downtime as
the Flagger struts its stuff.

No known natural predators
for this bothersome breed.
They continue to clog up
standard transportation routes,
causing delays and frustration
until winter migration arrives.

Dog Days of Summer

Blazin' bulldog.
Heated husky.
Lethargic labrador.
Perspired poodle.
Melted malamute.
Baked boxer.
Roasted rottweiler.
Cooked collie.
Desert dachshund.
Toasted terrier.
Scorched spaniel.
Balmy basset.
Seared shepherd.
Sweltered sheltie.
Dehydrated dalmatian.
Grilled greyhound.
Broiled beagle.
Wilted Weimaraner.

Parched pooches.
Hot dogs!

Memorial Day

Many consider it to be
an homage to freedom,
honoring brave soldiers
no longer with us –
praise for our protectors.

For others, the holiday is
an obligatory salute to the
memories of relatives gone.
Fresh flowers on each grave.
Annual commitment complete.

It's a three day weekend
to travel, picnic, camp out.
Relax. Play. Renew.
Get yard ready for summer.
Refrain from being too busy.

For me, it's a bit of all three,
more mentally than physically.
I think of my father serving
in the naval submarine division
as a reservist for twelve years.

Recall relatives who've passed.
My Mom, Dad and late wife.
Uncles, Aunts and Grandparents.
Set time aside to welcome
the memories they left behind.

It's also a day to savor the living.
Enjoy extra time with a partner.
Appreciate the abundance of love
appearing now, not in the past.
Occasion to enshrine both life and death.

Autumn

As summer spends
its last currency,
autumn arrives
with a new bankroll,
buying new colors
for trees and
bartering some
blue sky from
Mother Nature.

Days shorter,
evenings longer,
with cooler temperatures
providing a briskness
fitting with the
season's reputation.
Sweatshirts and jackets,
not used since spring –
necessary once again.

It's a time when
leaves wear their
final costumes
before descending
to earth,
abandoning abode –
gently gliding to the
ground below creating
branches bare, unclothed.

Autumn's swirling winds
blow them around like
red, brown and gold confetti –
an all out tickertape parade
celebrating color's
last hurrah before
bleakness of winter
arrives to pave its way
in white and gray.

Before Winter Arrives

Consummation of crisp air,
cuddling on moonlight hayride,
dimly lit with flickering lantern,
sipping on mug of hot apple cider
under cozy, warm wool blanket.

Ravens gone southward.
Time to take down scarecrow.
Stellar job, protecting the harvest.
Talents no longer required as rain, wind,
mist and fog, usher fall into winter.

We know she's coming.
As autumn winds down,
the trepidation of her arrival
colors our contentment while
preparing for her emergence.

With a frosty reception,
she's a house guest
who stays too long,
making a mess of
sidewalks and roadways.

Make new memories
before winter's entrance
in her mysterious white veil –
freezing all she touches
with cool, frigid, icy breath.

All Hallows Eve

Werewolf, Frankenstein,
Count Dracula and a mime.
Trick or treat in their duds.
All out for candy, not blood.

Pirate, scarecrow
know where to go.
Skeleton, Goblin
beg without robbin'.

Scary, spooky.
Monster mash cutie.
Mummy, ghost –
haunted house host.

Zombie, witch
magic wand switch.
Princess and prince
partied ever since.

A spell for one night –
purposeful fright.
Take to the streets.
Creepy gets the sweets.

Horn of Plenty

Symbolic, hollow horn
filled with inexhaustible
celebratory fruits and nuts.
Bounty of Autumn.

My Horn of Plenty
is metaphysical.
Metaphor of season's riches.
Figurative feast of Fall.

Vibrant foliage of amber,
reds and cinnamon browns.
College football traditions
in cool, crisp air.

Apple cider, corn mazes,
harvests and hayrides.
Cozy flannel shirt
suffices as a jacket.

Squirrels store their food
when gusty winds and frost
warn of a change toward
the coming winter.

Time for comfort foods.
Soup. Stew. Apple pie.
Spicy aroma of
kitchen's cloves and nutmeg.

Rake and blower round up
bushels of fallen leaves.
Deciduous branches barren
for viewing the evening moon.

Fireplace's warm embrace.
Gratitude for equinox migration.
Horn of Plenty – an inspiration.
Certainly not hollow at all.

Giving Thanks

Grateful for all
Thanksgivings –
past and present.

Love. Food.
Health. Humor.
Communion.

Be it with a
plethora of
kith and kin.

Or intimate affair.
Few – or just
me and you.

Enticing aroma
of roasting turkey
hours before we eat.

Teases appetite.
Hankering hunger
for upcoming feast.

Pleasantries
pass the time
before we dine.

Nearly always –
eyes bigger
than stomach.

Dessert finds room
even if there's none.
Reverse famine.

Celebration
lethargic when
tryptophan kicks in.

Thanksgiving Goodbye

Mom was dying.
Her heart could
no longer pump blood
strong enough for her legs.

Hospice came over –
taught dad how to
turn her by using
the bedsheets.

Both planned to
go to my sister's place
for Thanksgiving dinner.
It was not to be.

She could no longer walk.
Instead of joining them
at my sister's feast,
we would have one there.

Picked up the last
"complete turkey dinner"
from a grocery deli
thinking it would be a snap.

Unpacked it at
my parent's home –
realized it was uncooked.
Set oven to 325°.

Potatoes needed time.
So did corn, rolls, gravy
and for dessert, apple pie.
Dinner in four hours *(I hoped)*.

Cooking for Thanksgiving
not in my wheelhouse.
But remembered all those years
when Mom did it all, so perfectly.

When it was finally done,
I prepared all our plates,
placed on three TV trays
set next to the bed.

Sitting up with a few pillows,
Mom put on a smile –
began eating like it was
the best meal she ever had.

"Yum Yum," she declared
as her spoon scooped some corn.
soft mashed potatoes and
small cut up turkey pieces.

We talked as if we were
the same family who had
enjoyed Thanksgiving together
decades ago.

During those moments,
the immense sadness of
her deteriorating condition
all but disappeared.

It was Thanksgiving
as we all remembered.
Mom ate better
than she had in days.

Dad stayed in her room
while I cleared the plates,
finished carving turkey
and packed up leftovers.

The meal wasn't fancy
but it was shared with the
two people who brought me
into this world with their love.

Six days later, mom was gone.
Our last real Thanksgiving –
a sentimental send off
forever in my heart.

"Thanksgiving, man! Not a good day to be my pants."
 – Kevin James

Thanksgiving Pants

Thanksgiving, the reason
I rarely go to buffets.
Everything so delicious,
must have some of all of it
when the meal gets underway.

Pass the turkey, stuffing,
gravy, taters and rolls.
Even green bean casserole
gets a spot on the plate
while my diet is on parole.

Halfway through dining,
pants are far too tight.
Undo the top button –
down a notch on my belt.
Then it feels just right.

Just when I think I cannot
consume any more –
out comes pumpkin pie
with a scoop of ice cream
and I am all aboard.

Go from table to
the sofa for a nap.
Tryptophan puts me
in a sleepy-eyed coma –
Thanksgiving – that's a wrap!

Glad Tidings

That time of the year again –
bells rung, candles lit.
Most everyone is ritually festive.

Cookies decorated, eggnog made –
parade of parties offers tempting feasts,
increasing weight and waistlines.

Partridges, chestnuts and sugarplums
emerge in the seasonal vocabulary.
Wonder and wishes catch and release.

Advent. Yuletide pageant.
No matter nippy chills and icicles,
warmth of fellowship overflows.

Holly and mistletoe commemorate
heartfelt, human compassion.
Glad tidings given and received.

Fade too quickly – sadly temporary.
Charity and kindness, only a visitor,
skate away, as our hearts turn icy once again.

Dear Santa

I realize it's been
decades since I last
wrote you a letter.
My childhood wish
for a toy I saw on TV
or discovered in
the Sears Catalog
is no longer.

This Christmas,
in my 72nd year,
I wish for things
that might not be
in your endless
gift knapsack.
It could very well
puzzle the elves.

During this season
of giving and love,
I wish people
would realize
our differences
are minute
compared to all
we have in common.

Religiously,
what does it matter
which god or gods
we worship?
Doesn't it really
get down to just
being a good
caring person?

Politically,
we all want a country
that doesn't limit
our freedoms.
Gives us a fair shake.
Both parties are
different sides
of the same coin.

Humanly,
I wish we could
figure out how
not to kill each other
over jealousy, envy,
power, hunger, money.
Never a good war.
Never a bad peace.

We've come a long way
over the last century
dealing with discrimination
of race, bias, gender, age.
I wish we'd keep up
the progress and
continue compassion
of our social evolution.

I think about my grandchildren –
whether we are leaving
them a better world
than a generation before.
My wish is we somehow will.
My wish is for more love, less hate.
Let your Santa magic grant it.
You are needed more than ever.

The Naughty List

All year long –
worrying about
whether the
slightest infraction
could cause
it to happen.

Naughty list
recipients
would not get a
happy Christmas
with glorious gifts
and Santa's Ho Ho Ho.

Rumored
they receive
sticks or
lumps of coal
instead of
stocking stuffers.

Determined
by behavior.
How harsh the crime?
Does the Big Guy
separate felony
from misdemeanor?

You may
have stepped
on a crack –
and rushed home
to see if mother's
back was broken.

January would begin
with halos and
eventually slip
off the head
way before
December's trial.

All decided by
one plump elf
without the
aid of a jury,
witnesses or
legal representation.

Would being
extra nice
counteract
all the small
infractions and
minor malfeasance?

Maybe. Just maybe,
Santa didn't see the
snowball hit your sister.
Maybe he saw
all the times you
could have – but didn't.

No one knows
if they're on the
naughty list until
Christmas morning.
When stockings are full and
children's prayers answered.

Holiday Greetings

Charity. Goodwill.
Blessings. Grace.
Gifts. Giving.
Christmas spirit.
Epiphany embrace.

Family visits.
Log crackling aroma.
Hymns heard.
Too much cheer.
Hangover coma.

Cranberry merry.
Rejoice. Revere.
Candies. Cakes.
Waistline wider
this time of year.

Calorie abundance.
Festive laughter.
Tradition glistens.
Gingerbread stars.
Diet disaster.

Indulgence over
without relapse.
January arrives.
Holidays done.
Anticlimax.

I Believe in Angels

Advent ascent.
Time to focus on
holiday decorations
we can see and
spirits we cannot.

If it's true –
every time a bell rings,
an angel gets its wings –
there's certainly a
surplus at Christmas.

Time for glad tidings.
Gifts and goodwill.
Ceremonies, festivals,
candy canes and cake.
Traditions we celebrate.

Angels keep it merry.
Invisible, unobtrusive,
behind the scenes –
foster togetherness
and family fellowship.

Presents, twinkling lights –
even good ole St. Nick.
All part of that
soulful ember warmth
you feel in your heart.

They whisper to us that
there's more than the
superficial hype that
surrounds the season.
The miracle angels bring,

Bare Trees

You only see
bare trees
when you
winter visit.

More deciduous
than evergreen.
Naked branches
against gray sky.

You must think
it odd to live
among so many
wooden skeletons.

Without green –
black, tan, brown
seasonally survive in
sepia sensibility.

Come spring, when
bare becomes alive –
new growth
clothed in green.

Lush, this landscape.
Color shades in
expansive, luxurious
vision richness.

See us when
it's gloriously green.
Foliage and flora
undeniably opulent.

We are much more
than bare trees
seen through
your mind's winter lens.

Full Moon

Silverly light,
very bright,
shines the night
for batwings flight.

It's been said
rays raise the dead
from their permanent bed.
Or release crazy instead.

Werewolf. Vampire.
Full moon required.
Protective bonfire
does what's desired.

Changes the tide.
Affects feelings inside.
Intentions applied
with full moon ritual guide.

Animals and botany,
astronomical acrimony.
Lunar lunacy –
night without normalcy.

Giant Killer

Dinosaur trees,
the Sequoias.
Living survivor for
over 200 million years.

California lumberjacks
began slaying the giants
in mid 1800's for profit.
Like sperm whales.

"Mammoth Tree"
took a troop of men
three weeks to cut
through its trunk.

The 300 foot
1,244 year-old tree fell –
with a section of its bark
ending up on Broadway.

Days of PT Barnum
provided a market for
oohs and aahs for the
forthcoming freakshow.

So, more were cut.
One displayed at
London's Crystal Palace
in Victorian England.

Eighty-nine percent of all
the old growth annihilated.
Small groves of remaining
Sequoias now protected.

Except from nature.
Wildfires don't care
what fodder it flames.
A wood once used for matchsticks.

Groves grow smaller.
Like Jack (without lumber)
humanity lays an egg.
Loses its golden goose.

I Am Tree

Autumn now.
Green leaves
turning color,
dropping to
forest floor,
thinning my
protective cloak.

Soon, as all
leaves depart,
branches bare,
like skeleton bones,
prepare me
for long sleep
through winter.

Cold, stormy
winds blow
through
rather than
sway me
with its
persuasion.

It's a long,
lonely slumber,
but I am
resilient.
Spring will
signal me
to awaken.

And I will grow
new sprouts
that become
leaf attire
fit for
my majesty.
For I AM TREE.

Behind the Cloud

Metaphysical cloud
raining on my spirit –
spoiling my mood
and outlook
toward the future.

Turbulent times.
With little to
protect myself
from annoyance
and distress.

Sometimes it
feels hopeless.
Cumulonimbus.
Blowing gusts
with roaring thunder.

And me,
looking for shelter.
Any protection –
elusive illusory.
Lack of certainty.

Fortunately,
there is hope
beyond the cloud.
Beyond the storm.
Beyond the madness.

Winds of change
will blow in.
Better weather
with hope.
Optimism.

They say every cloud
has a silver lining.
Important to remember
there is blue sky
behind every cloud.

If we rise above it.

Daydream

Butterflies flutter
like flying flowers or
fairies without petals.

Daffodils and tulips
burst in a bloom
of colorful patterns.

Green grass and
cherry blossoms
donate their fragrance.

Thunderstorm provides
dramatic interruption of
nature's tranquility.

Robin sings delight
at morning sunrise,
waking all in earshot.

Arising from
indoor world,
longing the smell of spring.

There are only two ways to live your life. One is though nothing is a miracle. The other is though everything were a miracle.
– Albert Einstein

It's a Miracle

That
  love lives.
  humans heal.
  nature nurtures.
  consciousness conceives color.
  music's meaningful.
  sun shines.
  art allures.
  literature liberates.
  science serves.
  happiness happens.
  passion percolates.
  relationships remain.
  offspring occur.
  change continues.
  water is wonder.
  pets provide pleasure.
  heartbeats happen.
  souls survive.

Hibernation

Let's cocoon away –
winter's breath upon us.
Protection from beastly cold
and every frigid gust.

Time to take it easy.
Recuperate. Relax.
Far away from exposure
or unexpected attacks.

Cuddle in together –
warmth of ember glow.
Let our love linger –
relish sentiment slow.

Goodbye hustle bustle.
Hello slothful sleep.
Wind down heart and mind.
Slumber very deep.

When birds begin to sing
and flowers start to sprout,
abandon hidden hideaway –
see what the world's about.

Cold hearted orb that rules the night,
Removes the colors from our sight.
Red is grey and yellow white,
But we decide which is right.
And which is an illusion?
 – Graeme Edge *(Drummer for the Moody Blues)*

Moonlight Myopia

Moon
illuminates
and disguises
darkness.

Colors
disappear –
shadow world
revealed.

Nocturnal ones
awake –
welcome the
stealth cloak.

Cold hearted orb
does nothing
to warm
mother earth.

Instead,
pale gleam
teases with
reflective radiance.

Creating
hiding places
for the strange
and supernatural.

Lunar light lurks.
Laments it
cannot moan.
Or howl.

Fear of its
dim offering –
doubt, dread,
dismay.

Moonlight –
hand in hand
with blackness
and murky intentions.

Flower Greets Morning

Sun peeks out from horizon.
Awakens sleeping flower
to greet day's dawn.

Hello sun!
Good morning, sky.
I'm ready to open
my blossoms –
scent unfurled,
color the world.

My nectar –
ready for collectors.
Come bees and birds,
enter my flora –
extract all you require.
Much as you desire.

My way of spreading
new life, you see.
Pat my petals –
innocently transfer
personal pollination
to new destination.

Delay dalliance.
No matter the distance.
Existence requires
your persistence.
Flower sex
requires assistance!

"Sunsets are proof that endings can often be beautiful, too."
– Beau Taplin

Sunset

Does the sun drown
when it disappears
into the sea –
coloring
the horizon?

It does not.

Instead, it gives us
beautiful moments
of orange, red, pink
and purple hues
before its goodbye.

Parting gift.
Something to treasure.
Different masterpiece
each and every day,
fading before our eyes.

Is it an ending
as dusk melts
into darkness and
reveals the beyond
of planets and stars?

Or is it a dessert
to a glorious day?
Visual digestif
to cap our meal
of daylight.

An ending
that comes
with promise
of reappearance
and hope.

Indeed,
an exquisite departure.
Leaving its taste to linger –
far after moon rises
as its nightly stand-in.

New Mantra for Congress

Bold beginnings.
Bestow bravery.
Build bridges.
Bring balance.

Set boundaries.
Boost belonging.
Bar betrayal.
Block blame.

Belief –
benevolence
better than
bitterness.

Blessings
better than
blight and
bewilderment.

Sadly,
Congress broken.
Repair
beneath them.

Not about
the people,
but rather
the parties.

Best we can hope
for all the banality
is a brisk return
to mutual civility.

Working together,
there's no limit
on what can
be accomplished.

The future ain't what it used to be.
– Yogi Berra

The Future Falters

I am less hopeful
about the future
than I used to be.

I was praying
for more
promising prospects.

Fringe extremists
gain
in numbers.

Longer leisure.
30-hour
work weeks.

Common sense
becomes
more uncommon.

People
coming together
not drifting apart.

Professional
medical advice
ignored.

A world
where no one
goes hungry.

Election
integrity
doubted.

Not trickling
down debt
to our children.

Justice system
labeled unfair
and politicized.

Prejudice, bigotry
and intolerance
eliminated.

Inflation
eating into
savings.

Leaving our planet
a better place
than it was before.

Wars turning
security into a
ticking time bomb.

A future fantasy
still worth looking
forward to.

Moving Forward

The pendulum swings
in politics all the time.
Too much of one thing
counterbalances the other.

Migrating backwards in
women's reproductive rights –
welcoming new citizens –
intelligent political decorum.

Not only a Christian nation,
but a nation of many religions,
races, preferences, talents, abilities.
Melting pot called the U.S. of A.

Somehow, it works.
Our country – stronger for it.
Change is necessary to
move beyond the past.

Going backwards, a retreat
to a lesser civilized past.
Carnival barkers make it tempting.
Lure the impressionable in.

The genie cannot be put
back into the bottle.
Recreate life decades ago.
Nostalgia of nonsense.

Moving forward to
deal with new difficulties –
search for superior solutions –
build a better country.

Light a Candle for Freedom

There once was a time
when peaceful protest
was a legitimate legal way
to express dissatisfaction.
Now fear prevents action.

There once was a time
when facts and evidence
were methods to deal with
criminal behavior.
Except for a wannabe savior.

There once was a time
equality was a worthy pursuit
and acceptance was
considered a positive trait.
Today, evil and doubt tempt fate.

There once was a time
when facts were facts,
not blinded by
defiance and distortion.
Lies in ample portions.

There once was a time
when democracy was invulnerable,
existence never questioned.
Power without restraint done.
Light a candle for freedom.

Day of Reason

Just one day.
A day not hampered
by revenge on enemies
or completely partisan
attacks on institutions
held dear.

One day when tariffs
are just a bad dream.
When consumers don't
fear rising prices and
feel secure with their
retirement savings.

One day of reason.
A day when Ukraine
isn't blamed for the war
Russia clearly started.
Or fault former president Biden
for current stock market fluctuations.

One day when the president
doesn't make my stomach hurt,
as I'm eating my breakfast,
with his idiotic, untrue,
irrational late night comments
affecting the rest of my day.

Is one day of reason
too much to ask for?
A day of sunshine
before the world gets
covered by storm clouds?
A day when everyone sees clearly?

I pray for such a day.
When Moses parted the sea
to set people free.
To come together and celebrate
the good we have in common
versus debating our differences.

Era of My Ways

Wish I lived in an era
where prejudice didn't exist.
Migrants become citizens
without deportation fear.

An era where
homelessness is a word
banished from the dictionary
because all have abodes.

An era where politicians
assist constituents
instead of big pharma
or persuasive lobbyists.

An era where everyone
has opportunity, employment,
food on the table and
savings account in the bank.

An era where law enforcement
works hand in hand with
the public they serve –
appreciation on both sides.

An era where the very rich
built libraries and museums
instead of social media networks
and flights into space.

An era where job security
revered and valued –
gold watches given
after 40 years of service.

An era where
health and education
a primary right –
fairly distributed to all.

Unfortunately, it's an era
that doesn't exist –
and may never will.
Is it not a dream to strive for?

No man has a good enough memory to be a successful liar.
– Abraham Lincoln

Successful Liar

Remember which lie
told to which person –
keep the stories straight.
Sincerity – an invention.
Nothing to negate.

Fabrication. Fiction.
Falsehoods weave
wicked web of yarns.
Easier said than done
to set off no alarms.

Successful liars require
confidence and trust.
Believers to believe.
If no one knows the truth,
it's simple to deceive.

Ears hear forked tongue.
Saps. Suckers. Schmucks.
Dupes. Fools. Chumps.
Successful liars have the right words
until the day they're stumped.

When queries materialize.
Questions. Examinations.
Things simply don't add up.
Successful liar thwarted
when truth interrupts.

The Final Chapter

It has been said,
due to recent
election results,
we'll witness a
final end to our
experiment in
democracy.

Perhaps concerns
are overblown.
Anxiety needless.
Apprehension
unnecessary.
Worry and distress
unjustified.

On the other hand,
perhaps much to fear.
Bets hedged,
rules bent,
morality manipulated.
Needy impoverished.
Privileged power.

Little we can do
but watch the
republic unfold
into an entity
we couldn't
have imagined.
Or wished for.

Founding fathers
never conceived
the baffling scenario
we find ourselves in now.
Seismic activity
created by all of them
turning in their graves.

Will we survive?
Most likely.
Sun will still rise
in the east and
set in the west.
Our freedom –
clearly another question.

Mayday, Mayday

The plea when
trouble imminent –
rescue all.

This time,
democracy
makes the call.

When future
is mayhem –
country in dismay.

Maybe voters
become heroes
to save the day.

Preserve and
protect freedom.
No time for delay.

Desperate, dire
emergency that
won't go away.

"Mayday, mayday"
the republic
begs and prays.

May we be the
saviors to prevent
such decay.

Bamboozled

Duped by false accusations.
Deceived by denigrative remarks.
Asserted allegations unproven.
Hoodwinked in the dark.

Armed with the three "D's" –
deception, deflection, defamation.
Debacle assails authenticity
and confidence in our nation.

Some simply cannot see
the chicanery and coercion.
Blind to blatant hypocrisy –
covert claims and corruption.

Furor from the Führer.
Denies illegal aspirations.
Influence by bamboozle –
a fiasco of fabrications.

Attack on our democracy
for personal and financial gain.
Control and greed the benefit.
Embezzlement of truth – the game.

We don't want dictatorship
or a demagogue in the making.
Authoritarian rule illicit.
Naïve endorsement heartbreaking.

Surreal

We live in a traverse universe.
Where justice is perceived
by some as honest while
others call it a sham.

It must be one or the other.
Our fair system with rules,
evidence and peer judgement
proven worthy since it began.

Courts bad. Election stolen.
All because one side didn't
get their way. Reward a riot.
Shut down rule of law.

The aim is confusion.
Questions where there
shouldn't be any at all.
Civility hacked.

Searching for validation.
Illegible justification to
stomp the competition
with demented destruction.

Tearing down our legal institution
so it can be replaced with theirs
blackens our birthright –
spawns a fascist faith.

There'll be no democratic future
if such malicious efforts continue.
Brace for circling storms, gusty winds –
and batten down the hatches.

Resuscitation

Nearly out of breath –
the old order of things;
frail, feeble, fragile...
brought to life once more
by nostalgic believers.

Winds of change
don't blow
their direction.
Ignored. Rejected,
Avoided at all costs.

Status quo.
Familiar blanket,
worn and tattered.
Snuggled and nestled.
Satisfied with mundane.

But things do change.
Perceptions. Emotions.
Money. Technology.
Natural disasters.
Unnatural catastrophes.

So many of them
out of anyone's control.
We do not possess
the ability to
make time stand still.

In fact, time is the greatest
deterrent to the old order.
Eventually breathing
its last breath, no matter
what the attempts.

We live in a world going
one step forward while some
purposely take one step back.
Breathing in stale air
of their own demise.

Trumpty Dumpty

Populous duped.
Bad egg won.
Egg on our face as
we plunge into dung.

Checks and balances
held in contempt.
All eggs in one basket
becomes the intent.

Revenge on enemies
who simply disagree.
Walking on eggshells
instantly mandatory.

Needs no one
to egg him on.
Opposite of truth –
his only song.

Man with matches.
Sits on powder keg.
Kills the goose, yet still
expects the golden egg.

Hard boiled atrocities
saddened and sobbed.
Democracy in peril.
Nest egg robbed.

All our resources
and all our amends
couldn't stop Dumpty
from lying again.

Plum Dandy

Checks and balances
lobsided, out-of-whack.
Plum dandy.

President setting
poor precedents.
Plum dandy.

Executive orders
from Russian supporter.
Plum dandy.

Enemies made
of former friends.
Plum dandy.

ICE deporting
regular citizens.
Plum dandy.

Tariffs – must
grin and bear it.
Plum dandy.

Stock market
plunges trillions.
Plum dandy.

Tax breaks for
the very rich.
Plum dandy.

Cutting vital
social services.
Plum dandy.

Emergency powers
without a crisis.
Plum dandy.

Turning from
"hi ya" to pariah.
Plum dandy.

Rotten apple
spoils the bunch.
Plum dandy.

Good of it
not so much.
Plum dandy.

Even though
we're told that it is.
It's really Plum Crazy.

Jack Smith

Footnote in history.
Purveyor for truth.
Evidence of misdeeds.
Collected all the proof.

Gave his honest best to
bring notice to the crimes.
Witchhunt! cried the adversary.
And on the government's dime!

Confounded by goal posts
moving further and further away.
Rule of law weakened.
Justice a cliché.

The one thing achieved –
pandora's box unlocked.
Equal punishment for everyone –
certainly a crock.

Prosecution, no solution
to the powerful and rich.
Duck and weave, Delay, delay.
Free without a hitch.

Thank you, Jack –
honest man in a crooked game.
Wish it turned out differently.
I'm sure he feels the same.

Tarriff Sheriff

He decides just what rate
each country should pay –
and what products effected.
Justification?
Because he was elected.

Tariffs on this and that
makes government coffers fat.
Or so the sheriff said.
All that money coming in –
profitable way to get ahead.

That's only half the story –
which steals the sheriff's glory.
The one who coughs up
the new tariff extra expense –
the consumer, if that makes sense.

Countries that buy from us
don't need a tariff adjust.
Wheat, soybeans, even cars –
they'll simply look elsewhere,
leaving export sales sparse.

The on/off switch in Sheriff's hands
U-turns too much to understand.
One step forward, two steps back,
the great negotiator vacillates
while the rest of the world reacts.

Enemies created from allies.
Trade deficit multiplies.
Sheriff forces clout like a bully.
Shootout at the OK Corral.
Our good name used disgracefully.

Misinformation

Disguise of lies.
Cobweb of dishonesty.
Hyperbole hubbub.
Flimflam falsehoods.
Steadfast subterfuge.

Truth in toilet.
Barefaced lies.
Subtle shenanigans.
Facts in shambles.
Validity flabbergasted.

Highfalutin bigwigs
bend the genuine to fit
hoity-toity fanfare.
Hogwash served up
on a silver platter.

A crime to spiel
such ballyhoo.
Behavior of
criminals and hoodlums.
And now, politicians.

Trumpery ABCs

Absurd
Bogus
Childish
Deluded
Exaggerator
Fake
Groper
Hoodwinker
Inappropriate
Jester
Kooky
Ludicrous
Malarkey
Nonsensical
Ogler
Phony
Quibbler
Ridiculous
Shallow
Tacky
Unaccountable
Victimizer
Wacky
X-president
Yowler
Zealot

Tattered and Frayed

American flag.
Symbol of freedom.
Truth and justice.
Equality. Integrity.
Liberty.

It's been
going through
tough times.
Challenged.
Questioned.

Leaving
stars and stripes
tattered. Frayed.
Battle scars.
Edges – threads.

Yet, still
waves in wind
for more than
two hundred years
of democracy.

Maligned.
Rejected. Scorned.
As it has by some
throughout
our history.

No matter
the challenge,
it overcomes
adversity.
Triumphs.

It still stands.
Despite social strife
or trepid turbulence.
Steadfast.
Our salvation.

Our guardian.
Flexing. Flying.
Bending with the times.
Protector of nation.
Defender of what we hold dear.

Peace

It was how we greeted each other
during the Summer of Love:
The peace sign.
It said hello. Or goodbye.
To strangers or friends.
It meant
we were on the same wavelength.

We'd say *"peace"* or
"peace, brother" (or sister)
as our formal introduction.
There was a war on.
Americans dying in the
jungles of Vietnam.
We were against it.

Incorporating our politics
into ordinary daily life.
Commonality of disgust
at the government's involvement
in a foreign dispute –
sacrificing young soldiers.
For what?

Perhaps we should resurrect
the conversation again.
Make the peace sign
a universal greeting –
the first topic of discussion.
We have the right to do so.
And it's more likely to happen if we do.

Peace.

Why Dogs Hate Cats

Everyone knows dogs hate cats. And cats aren't too crazy about canines, either. Sure, there are some rare exceptions of friendliness toward one another, but let's face it, overall there is no love lost between them. If you never knew exactly what happened to cause this disdain, then this is the story for you.

A long time ago, when humans decided to start adopting dogs and cats and allowing them into their home, everything was great. Dog or Cat or both would snuggle up to the cozy fire and enjoy the dinner table scraps.

In the wild, a dog would catch a rabbit or squirrel and sometimes eat a dead fish washed up on the shore. A cat would eat mice. A rat if it was small enough. A bird if it was slow enough. Then they would seek some sort of shelter – a small cave, a hollow fallen tree or a thick briar – to withstand the elements of heat, cold, rain and snow. And to protect themselves from prey which might enjoy a delicious dog or cat for a nice little snack.

But all that changed when the humans made them pets. They didn't have to worry about shelter because they now lived in a human home. They didn't have to worry about finding food or water because the humans fed them. And each enjoyed the protection of the human home, as it kept them safe from other animals who wanted to eat them. Yep, it was a pretty good deal. Certainly, something that neither one of them wanted to screw up.

Now, Cat figured out this free ride even faster than Dog. Since it still enjoyed catching mice and eating them, it wasn't all that difficult to catch some mice in this friendly new shelter. In fact, it was a cinch. And when their humans saw what Cat was doing, they liked it very much. They thanked the cat. Gave it a special treat.

Once Cat realized it pleased the humans so much, it kept the home mouse free. When one of the humans was sitting down for a rest, it hopped up on the lap and curled up in a ball. When the human ran its hands lightly upon the cat's fur, Cat purred. The human liked that sound. So, Cat figured it would catch mice and purr when people petted it. Then it could simply sleep the rest of the time. It was an easy gig and Cat knew it.

And nothing – or no one – was going to spoil this perfect setup. Dog, on the other hand, didn't know what his tasks would be in the home. At first, it tried to copy Cat, which predictably didn't work out so well. It couldn't catch mice worth a darn and wasn't welcome on the human lap. And it couldn't purr. But it could bark. When it heard something strange or smelled something new, it would bark and bark and bark. The human would go see what the commotion was about, come back and pet it on its fur. So now it knew how it could please humans too. Barking is easy, Dog thought. The rest of the time, it slept in the warm home.

But that changed rather quickly. The man human took Dog with him outside to hunt. It took it a little while, but when Dog figured out how to point out game in a manner that didn't disturb it, the human liked that VERY much. Besides, it was fun to go outside, smell all the smells and run about the countryside.

Cat didn't like all this human attention going to Dog. It was especially disgusted with a new game Dog and the male human played called "fetch." The human would throw a stick and Dog would bring it back. They would do it again and again and again. Cat hoped it would never have to play that stupid game. Ever.

Suddenly the home felt smaller and more crowded to Cat. Dog was getting a lot more attention and its fur got petted more than ever. Dog's big tongue would stick out as it smiled and that taunted Cat tremendously.

One day, when Dog was hunting with its human, Cat came upon a very large rat. Rat was scared, but Cat had other plans. It told Rat about how Dog was invading its life and took lap time away from its humans. If Rat would help it get rid of Dog, Cat promised it would not bother Rat and both could live peacefully together.

The dinner soup was cooling in the kitchen and Cat had an idea. When the humans were in another room, Rat would push one of the bowls off the counter, spilling soup on the floor. Cat would be with the humans, so it would not be suspected. And Rat would disappear quickly as well, leaving only one animal to blame.

Dog had arrived home and the plan was put into action. It couldn't have worked out more perfectly. Cat was with the humans, the bowl was knocked over and when the humans came into the kitchen, they found Dog licking delicious soup up off the floor. Dog was put outside after a good yelling. It was confused and very sad. The next day, the male human built Dog a new dwelling, called a doghouse. Now Dog stayed outside most of the time and Cat had the inside all to itself. Cat was so happy, it purred and purred and purred.

Dog was confused. It used to be able to go inside the house and curl up to the nice warm fire. Now it had to stay outside in its own little house, which wasn't nearly as comfortable. But if that's what the humans wanted, it would do it. It still got table scraps and water, only outside now. Dog could see Cat through the window, lying on its human's lap. Cat seemed so contented.

One day, Dog came upon Rat by its doghouse. Rat had never seen a dog before and was even more scared of Dog than Cat. But Dog did not want to hurt Rat. It told Rat not to be scared – and if it liked, it could share his doghouse with him. Rat liked Dog and appreciated its kindness. Rat told Dog about Cat's plan to get rid of him and how Cat made Rat tip the bowl of soup on the floor. Dog was furious! It thought Cat was his friend. It felt betrayed. And angry.

As time went by, Dog was allowed back into the home, but only for short periods of time. Then back out to the doghouse it went. During one of its short visits, Dog asked Cat why it would do such a thing? Cat denied it, of course. But then Dog told Cat that Rat told it the whole sordid story. Cat just smiled at Dog and told it how much nicer the home has been since Dog now lives in the doghouse. Dog decided it didn't like Cat very much. In fact, it hated Cat. And it started chasing Cat around the house, only to be put back outside even quicker than usual.

Cat was coy the next time it saw Rat. Cat asked it how it had been and if it had been getting enough to eat. Rat said yes, the home was most comfortable. And then, Cat ate Rat. Since Rat was a pretty large one, Cat brought the remains to the woman human, who gave Cat a nice bowl of milk as a reward.

So, now you know why dogs hate cats. And why it never pays to be a rat.

Zippy, the cat, and Harley, the dog. Inspiration for Why Dogs Hate Cats.
Photo by Donna Lange

You can contact the author and learn about
Edmond Bruneau's other poetry books
and musical lyrics by going to
www.edmondbruneau.com

www.ingramcontent.com/pod-product-compliance
Lightning Source LLC
Chambersburg PA
CBHW041929090426
42744CB00016B/1994